TOMORROW'S TYCOONS: GEN Z AND THE UNPRECEDENTED WEALTH TRANSFER

(How Gen Z's Different Attitudes Towards Money and Power Will Save or Ruin the World)

Alfred S. Brown

INTRODUCTION: The Great Wealth Transfer: Making Preparations for the Unprecedented Transfer of Assets to Generation Z

While the Baby Boomer generation, which includes people born between 1946 and 1964, is beginning to hand over the reins of wealth to younger developing generations, notably Generation Z (Gen Z), which includes those born between 1997 and 2012, the globe is on the verge of seeing a wealth transfer that has never been seen before. It is anticipated that this wealth transfer will be the greatest in the history of the world, with an estimated thirty trillion dollars' worth of assets being passed from the Baby Boomers to Generation Z and other younger generations. This vast transfer of money will have far-reaching effects, including the restructuring of the global economy, the redefinition of wealth and power, and the development of new possibilities for innovation, growth, and social impact. These events will take place as a result of the transfer of wealth.

The extent of the wealth transfer, the forces that are driving it, and how Generation Z is ready to take on the responsibility of managing this unprecedented amount of money are all topics that will be discussed in this portion of the book. In addition, we shall investigate the difficulties.

In addition to the possibilities that come along with this transfer of wealth, as well as how it will influence the future of capitalism, social inequality, and economic development.

The Great Wealth Transfer: An Overview of the Situation

Over the course of many decades, a phenomenon known as the Great Wealth Transfer has manifested itself in a manner that is both intricate and varied. It is the outcome of a confluence of demographic, economic, and technical variables that have been responsible for the creation of a time in history that is unlike any other. Some of the primary factors of this transfer of wealth include:

1. Demographic changes: As the Baby Boomer group hits retirement age, they will begin to pass their money to younger generations, particularly Gen Z.

2. Increased lifetime: Advances in medical technology and healthcare have led to an increase in human lifespan, resulting in a bigger pool of rich persons hitting retirement age.

3. technology advancements: The quick speed of technology progress has offered new possibilities for wealth generation, as well as new means to manage and transfer assets.

4. Changing attitudes and beliefs: As society becomes more socially and ecologically aware, there is a rising realization of the need for more sustainable and responsible wealth management strategies.

The estimated $30 trillion in assets that will be transferred from the Baby Boomers to Gen Z and other younger generations is a significant increase from the $10 trillion transfer that took place between the Silent Generation (born 1928-1945) and the Baby Boomer generation. This signifies an almost 300% increase in the amount of money that will be transmitted between generations in the future decades.

The Wealth Transfer in Context: Why It Matters

The Great Wealth Transfer is not merely a financial event, but a cultural and sociological phenomenon with far-reaching implications. As the Baby Boomers transfer their money to younger generations, they will be passing on not just their financial holdings but also their values, beliefs, and experiences. This will provide new possibilities for intergenerational cooperation and knowledge transfer, as well as new problems for managing and preserving wealth.

The Great Wealth Transfer will also dramatically influence the global economy and financial markets. As the transfer of wealth takes place, it is expected to lead to changes in the balance of economic power, with developing markets and younger generations playing a more major role in global politics.

The transfer of wealth will also have profound social and cultural ramifications. As younger generations take on greater money and power, they will have the chance to impact society and culture in new and inventive ways. This might lead to a change in power relations, with younger generations having a more major role in molding the future of society and the economy.

Why This Generation Has the Potential to Become the Wealthiest in History

The Great Wealth Transfer, a phenomenon projected to take place in the next decades, is a once-in-a-lifetime chance for the next generation to establish a more sustainable and fair future. As the Baby Boomer generation, born between 1946 and 1964, starts to transfer an estimated $30 trillion in assets to younger generations, Generation Z (Gen Z), born between 1997 and 2012, has the potential to become the richest generation in history. In this chapter, we will investigate the reasons why Gen Z is set to inherit the greatest transfer of wealth and why this might lead to unparalleled economic development and social impact.

1. Gen Z's Technological Advantage:

Gen Z has grown up in a world of fast technological breakthroughs, with access to the internet and cell phones from a young age. This has given them a significant edge in understanding and utilizing emerging technology, which will play a major role in the creation of new businesses and services. As a consequence, Gen Z is likely to produce and invest in novel technology, leading to improved productivity and economic growth.

2. Environmental Consciousness:

Unlike earlier generations, Gen Z has been nurtured in a society where environmental concern is mainstream. As a consequence, they are more inclined to emphasize sustainability and social responsibility when it comes to financial management. This might lead to the creation of new companies and technology focused on tackling global concerns such as climate change, offering new chances for economic growth and innovation.

3. Diversity and Inclusion:

Gen Z is the most diverse generation in history, with many identifying as non-binary, genderqueer, or belonging to other oppressed groups. This variety brings fresh views and ideas to the table, which might lead to more inclusive and creative forms of wealth generation. As a consequence, Gen Z may be more willing to invest in socially responsible and diversified enterprises, leading to economic development and social impact.

4. Shift in Focus:

As the Great prosperity Transfer takes place, Gen Z's priority will move from financial prosperity to social effect. They are more inclined to emphasize utilizing their riches to achieve beneficial social and environmental change, rather than merely collecting things. This might lead to a more sustainable and equal distribution of wealth, with a stronger focus on long-term value generation.

5. Collaborative Spirit:

Gen Z is noted for its collaborative and community-focused attitude to living. As they inherit riches, they are likely to engage with others to build new partnerships and projects that benefit society as a whole. This might lead to more communal and collaborative forms of wealth generation, with a greater focus on helping local communities and social causes.

6. Generational Dynamics:

The Great Wealth Transfer will take place at a moment of enormous social and political change. Gen Z is likely to be more aware of these developments and more interested in leveraging their money to solve social and environmental concerns. As a consequence, they may be more willing to invest in programs that promote diversity, inclusion, and social justice, resulting in a more equal distribution of wealth.

The Great Wealth Transfer gives a great chance for Gen Z to achieve a more sustainable and fair future. With their technical edge, environmental conscience, diversity, inclusion, change in emphasis, collaborative spirit, and generational dynamics, they have the potential to become the richest generation in history. By emphasizing social impact and sustainable wealth creation, Gen Z can lead the way in crafting a better future for themselves and future generations.

The Challenges and Opportunities Ahead for Gen Z

The Great Wealth Transfer, a phenomenon predicted to take place in the future decades, poses both obstacles and possibilities for Generation Z (Gen Z). As the Baby Boomer generation, born between 1946 and 1964, continues to transfer an estimated $30 trillion in assets to younger generations, Gen Z, born between 1997 and 2012, will need to handle this unprecedented transfer of wealth. In this chapter, we will discuss the possible difficulties and possibilities ahead for Gen Z, including managing an unprecedented amount of money, tackling social and environmental concerns, and defining the future of capitalism.

1. Managing an Unprecedented Amount of Wealth:

Regardless of their financial strategy, Gen Z will be receiving a large amount of cash from the Baby Boomer generation. This transfer of wealth will generate new chances for innovation and prosperity, but it also carries the danger of ruining a generation. Gen Z will need to be careful of not just managing their riches but also ensuring that they utilize their resources ethically and sustainably.

2. Addressing Societal and Environmental Issues:

As the richest generation in history, Gen Z will have the potential to solve some of the world's most urgent socioeconomic and environmental concerns. They will need to emphasize their beliefs and invest in projects that promote diversity, inclusiveness, and social justice. Gen Z will also need to consider the environmental effect of their investments, as the globe confronts a climate catastrophe that demands quick care.

3. Shaping the Future of Capitalism:

As the Great Wealth Transfer takes place, Gen Z will have the chance to influence the future of capitalism. They will need to evaluate not just financial returns but also the social and environmental consequences of their investments. Gen Z will also need to think imaginatively about new forms of wealth production and distribution, since classic methods of capitalism may no longer be applicable in a quickly changing world.

4. Diverse Investment Strategies:

Gen Z is the most diverse generation in history, with many identifying as non-binary, genderqueer, or belonging to other oppressed groups. This variety brings fresh views and ideas to the table, which might lead to more inclusive and creative forms of wealth generation. Gen Z may opt to invest in sectors and firms that value diversity and inclusion, resulting to a more equal allocation of wealth.

5. Impact Investing:

Gen Z is more likely to emphasize socially responsible and sustainable investment, with an emphasis on producing good social and environmental impact. They may opt to invest in programs that address problems such as climate change, racial injustice, and gender equality, leading to a more sustainable and equitable future.

6. Philanthropy and Charitable Giving:

Gen Z is more inclined to emphasize philanthropy and charity giving, with an emphasis on supporting organizations that correspond with their beliefs. They may choose to give back to their communities via many types of philanthropy, including giving to local organizations, volunteering their time, and supporting social and environmental concerns.

7. Collaborative Spirit:

Gen Z is noted for its collaborative and community-focused attitude to living. As they inherit riches, they may choose to engage with others to build new partnerships and projects that benefit society as a whole. This might lead to more communal and collaborative forms of wealth generation, with a greater focus on helping local communities and social causes.

8. Shaping the Future of Work:

As the Great Wealth Transfer takes place, Gen Z will have the potential to redefine the future of labor. They may opt to invest in sectors and organizations that promote flexibility, remote work, and other kinds of work-life balance. This might lead to a more sustainable and fair future for the workforce, with a stronger focus on mental health and well-being.

CHAPTER 1: The Minds Behind the Movement

The Great Wealth Transfer is not merely a phenomena of enormous wealth transfer, but also a profound transformation in the way money is produced, managed, and dispersed. At the center of this transition are the Gen Z entrepreneurs, innovators, and leaders who are upsetting established businesses and generating new chances for social impact. In this chapter, we will study the brains behind the movement, emphasizing the fundamental features and attributes that identify this generation and their approach to wealth development.

The Gen Z Entrepreneurial Spirit

Gen Z is the most entrepreneurial generation in history, with a strong desire to forge their own path and make a significant effect on society. They are more likely to create their own enterprises, rather than working for someone else, and are more likely to disrupt existing sectors with novel technology and new business models. According to a recent poll, 75% of Gen Z entrepreneurs are inspired by the desire to have a good influence on society, showcasing their socially conscious approach to business.

The Rise of the Creative Class

In addition to their business drive, Gen Z is also defined by their inventiveness and creative thinking. They are more likely to seek employment in creative sectors such as art, design, and technology, and are more inclined to support diversity and inclusiveness in their workplaces. According to a new poll, 65% of Gen Z workers consider diversity and inclusion when selecting a job, indicating their dedication to building a more equal and inclusive workplace.

The Future of Work

As automation, AI, and remote work continue to impact the contemporary economy, Gen Z is well-positioned to handle these changes and create new possibilities for themselves and their peers. They are more inclined to accept flexible work arrangements and remote work, and are more likely to seek jobs in industries such as computing and entrepreneurship, which provide greater options for remote work and flexible scheduling. According to a recent poll, 55% of

Gen Z workers choose remote work, reflecting their desire for work-life balance and flexibility.

Key Takeaways:

* Gen Z is the most enterprising and creative generation in history, with a strong desire to establish their own path and make a significant effect on society.

* Gen Z is more likely to establish their own enterprises, disrupt existing sectors, and accept flexible work arrangements and remote employment.

* Gen Z is well-positioned to negotiate the changes brought about by automation, AI, and remote work, and create new possibilities for themselves and their peers.

The Great Wealth Transfer is not merely a phenomena of enormous wealth transfer, but also a profound transformation in the way money is produced, managed, and dispersed. At the center of this transition are the Gen Z entrepreneurs, innovators, and leaders who are upsetting established businesses and generating new chances for social impact. By studying the brains behind the movement, we may obtain insights into the essential features and attributes that distinguish this generation and their attitude to wealth creation, and how they might be helped to build a more sustainable and fair future for themselves and future generations.

CHAPTER 2: The Network Effect - How Gen Z Will Connect and Collaborate

The Great Wealth movement is not merely a movement of money resources, but also a transfer of information, ideas, and relationships. At the center of this transition is the Gen Z generation, who are more linked than ever before via digital technology. This connection has produced a new age of cooperation and collective intelligence, where Gen Z can harness the knowledge of the many to build a more sustainable and fair future. In this chapter, we will investigate how Gen Z will interact and cooperate, emphasizing the fundamental features and attributes that identify this generation and their approach to wealth creation.

Building a City on a Hill: The Rise of Digital Communities and Collective Intelligence

Gen Z is more likely to communicate with people via digital means, such as social media platforms, online forums, and messaging applications. These digital communities give a forum for members to exchange ideas, cooperate on projects, and support one another in their personal and professional goals. According to a recent poll, 70% of Gen Z members of digital community report feeling more connected to their peers as a consequence of these communities, showing the relevance of these networks in defining their attitude to wealth creation.

The Power of the Crowd: How Gen Z Will Harness the Wisdom of the Many

Gen Z is more prone to accept the wisdom of the crowd, seeking advice and feedback from a varied collection of people before making significant choices. This method of decision-making is assisted by digital technology, which give a forum for members to communicate their ideas and thoughts. According to a recent poll, 60% of Gen Z entrepreneurs seek input from their peers before making crucial choices, indicating their dedication to collaborative decision-making.

The Intersection of Technology and Humanity: How Gen Z Will Create New Forms of Collaboration

Gen Z is more inclined to embrace the convergence of technology and humans, producing new kinds of cooperation that integrate the best of both worlds. This approach to collaboration is characterized by an emphasis on empathy, creativity, and inclusion, and is aided by digital technologies that give a platform for members to interact and communicate. According to a recent poll, 55% of Gen Z entrepreneurs feel that technology and people should be blended to develop new kinds of cooperation, indicating their dedication to this strategy.

Key Takeaways:

* Gen Z is more likely to connect with others via digital means, establishing new types of digital communities and collective intelligence.

* Gen Z is more inclined to accept the wisdom of the crowd, seeking input and feedback from a varied range of people before making crucial choices.

* Gen Z is more likely to embrace the convergence of technology and humans, producing new forms of cooperation that integrate the best of both worlds.

The Great Wealth Transfer is not merely a phenomena of enormous wealth transfer, but also a profound transformation in the way money is produced, managed, and dispersed. At the center of this transition are the Gen Z entrepreneurs, innovators, and leaders who are upsetting established businesses and generating new chances for social impact. By understanding how Gen Z will connect and collaborate, we can gain insights into the key characteristics and traits that define this generation and their approach to wealth creation, and how they can be supported to create a more sustainable and equitable future for themselves and future generations.

CHAPTER 3: From Emoji to IPO - The Brilliant Minds and Bold Ventures of Gen Z

The Great Wealth movement is not merely a movement of money resources, but also a transfer of information, ideas, and innovation. At the center of this transition is the Gen Z generation, who are more likely to establish their own enterprises, disrupt existing sectors, and create new prospects for social impact. In this chapter, we will study the great brains and brave endeavors of Gen Z, emphasizing the fundamental features and attributes that distinguish this generation and their approach to wealth creation.

The Unicorn Maker: How Gen Z Will Build the Next Generation of Billion-Dollar Startups

Gen Z is more likely to create their own enterprises, and are more likely to disrupt existing sectors with breakthrough technology and new business models. According to a recent poll, 60% of Gen Z entrepreneurs are inspired by the goal to produce a game-changing product or service, reflecting their emphasis on innovation and disruption. Gen Z is also more likely to seek money from venture capitalists, angel investors, and crowdfunding sites, rather than conventional bank loans. According to a recent poll, 70% of Gen Z entrepreneurs say that angel investors and crowdfunding platforms are the most effective sources of funding for their enterprises, demonstrating their readiness to seek out alternative kinds of finance.

The Scale-Up Playbook: How Gen Z Will Structure and Grow Their Businesses

Gen Z is more likely to organize their enterprises in a manner that allows for sustainable development and scalability. This strategy is defined by an emphasis on efficiency, automation, and data-driven decision-making, and is assisted by digital technology that give real-time insights into corporate performance. According to a recent poll, 65% of Gen Z entrepreneurs utilize performance analytics tools to analyze their company development and performance, indicating their dedication to data-driven decision-making.

The VCs of Tomorrow: How Gen Z Will Invest, Influence, and Disrupt Venture Capital

Gen Z is more likely to invest in and influence the venture capital business, offering new chances for financing and development. According to a recent poll, 50% of Gen Z entrepreneurs feel that venture capital is a significant source of funding for their enterprises, demonstrating their readiness to seek out conventional means of finance. Gen Z is also more likely to disrupt the conventional venture capital paradigm, producing new forms of finance and investing that are more accessible and inclusive. According to a recent poll, 45% of Gen Z entrepreneurs feel that alternative types of finance, such as crowdsourcing and angel investing, are more significant than conventional venture capital, indicating their dedication to establishing a more varied and inclusive investment environment.

Key Takeaways:

* Gen Z is more likely to establish their own firms, disrupt existing sectors, and create new prospects for social influence.

* Gen Z is more likely to seek money from unconventional sources, such as venture capitalists, angel investors, and crowdfunding platforms.

* Gen Z is more likely to organize their enterprises in a manner that allows for sustainable development and scalability.

The Great Wealth Transfer is not merely a phenomena of enormous wealth transfer, but also a profound transformation in the way money is produced, managed, and dispersed. At the center of this transition are the Gen Z entrepreneurs, innovators, and leaders who are upsetting established businesses and generating new chances for social impact. By understanding the brilliant minds and bold ventures of Gen Z, we can gain insights into the key characteristics and traits that define this generation and their approach to wealth creation, and how they can be supported to create a more sustainable and equitable future for themselves and future generations.

CHAPTER 4: The Impact of Wealth on Society and Culture

The Great Wealth movement is not merely a movement of money resources, but also a transfer of attitudes, beliefs, and cultural traditions. At the center of this shift is the Gen Z generation, who are more inclined to utilize their riches to make good social effect and change the cultural environment. In this chapter, we will examine the ways in which Gen Z will utilize their riches to achieve good change, and how they will affect art, music, and culture.

The Rise of the New Philanthropy: How Gen Z Will Give Back

Gen Z is more inclined to utilize their income to produce good social effect, rather than merely contributing to established nonprofits. According to a recent poll, 75% of Gen Z donors prefer to fund local groups and projects, rather than huge, established nonprofits. This trend towards more hyperlocal giving reflects Gen Z's emphasis on community and diversity, and their desire to have a significant influence on the world around them.

The Future of Luxury and Consumption: How Gen Z Will Redefine the Meaning of Material Wealth

Gen Z is more inclined to rethink the meaning of financial riches, valuing experiences and relationships above commodities and prestige. According to a recent poll, 60% of Gen Z luxury customers emphasize sustainability and ethical sourcing when making purchase choices, reflecting their dedication to create a more equal and sustainable future. This trend towards more conscious consumerism reflects Gen Z's emphasis on values and purpose, and their desire to connect their buying patterns with their own ideals.

The Shape of Things to Come: How Gen Z Will Influence Art, Music, and Culture

Gen Z is more likely to alter the cultural environment via their distinct viewpoints and experiences. According to a recent poll, 70% of Gen Z creatives feel that their work has the capacity to inspire good change, showcasing their dedication to utilizing their art and creativity to have a significant influence on the world. This emphasis on harnessing creativity for good reflects Gen Z's ambition to utilize their riches and power to build a more inclusive, egalitarian, and sustainable future.

Key Takeaways:

* Gen Z is more inclined to utilize their income to produce good social effect, rather than merely contributing to established nonprofits.

* Gen Z is more inclined to rethink the meaning of financial riches, valuing experiences and relationships above commodities and prestige.

* Gen Z is more likely to impact the cultural environment via their unique viewpoints and experiences, utilizing their art and creativity to encourage good change.

The Great Wealth Transfer is not merely a phenomena of enormous wealth transfer, but also a profound transformation in the way money is produced, managed, and dispersed. At the center of this transition are the Gen Z entrepreneurs, innovators, and leaders who are upsetting established businesses and generating new chances for social impact. By understanding the ways in which Gen Z will use their wealth to create positive social impact, and how they will influence art, music, and culture, we can gain insights into the key characteristics and traits that define this generation and their approach to wealth creation, and how they can be supported to create a more sustainable and equitable future for themselves and future generations.

CHAPTER 5: The Changing Nature of Power and Influence

The Great Wealth movement is not merely a movement of money resources, but also a shift of power and influence. At the center of this transition is the Gen Z generation, who are more prone to question established structures of power and utilize technology to magnify their voices. In this chapter, we will examine the ways in which Gen Z will utilize their unique viewpoints and experiences to upend established systems of power and influence, and how they will define the attributes of effective leaders in the future.

The Great Reversal: How Gen Z Will Upend the Traditional Hierarchies of Power

Gen Z is more inclined to question established hierarchies of power, trying to create a more egalitarian and inclusive allocation of influence. According to a recent study, 75% of Gen Z respondents agree that power should be dispersed more evenly among people and organizations, indicating their dedication to establishing a more democratic and participatory society. This trend towards more diffused forms of authority reflects Gen Z's emphasis on cooperation, inclusiveness, and communal decision-making.

The Rise of the Faceless: How Gen Z Will Use Technology to Amplify Their Voices

Gen Z is more likely to utilize technology to enhance their voices and establish new kinds of influence. According to a recent poll, 60% of Gen Z respondents say that social media is the most effective method of communication, emphasizing the significance of digital platforms in defining their attitude to power and influence. This concentration on digital communication reflects Gen Z's desire to connect with people and build a more participative and inclusive society.

The Future of Leadership: How Gen Z Will Define the Traits of Successful Leaders

Gen Z is more inclined to describe successful leaders as people who exemplify a unique collection of skills and abilities, including empathy, inventiveness, flexibility, and a dedication to social impact.

According to a recent poll, 70% of Gen Z respondents feel that leaders should exhibit a strong sense of empathy and emotional intelligence, underscoring the significance of interpersonal skills in developing their approach to leadership. This emphasis on empathy and emotional intelligence reflects Gen Z's goal to establish a more caring and compassionate society, where leaders prioritize the interests of their constituents and stakeholders.

Key Takeaways:

* Gen Z is more inclined to question established systems of power and utilize technology to magnify their voices.

* Gen Z is more likely to identify successful leaders as individuals who exemplify empathy, innovation, flexibility, and a dedication to social impact.

* Gen Z is more likely to establish new kinds of influence and power, reflecting their dedication to cooperation, inclusiveness, and communal decision-making.

CHAPTER 6: The Ethics of Wealth and Success

The Great Wealth movement is not merely a movement of cash resources, but also a transfer of ideals and ethical principles. At the center of this shift is the Gen Z generation, who are more inclined to reinterpret the measures of success and failure, and combine individualism with communal duty. In this chapter, we will discuss the ways in which Gen Z will judge success and failure, and how they will traverse the trap of entitlement.

The Moral Compass of Gen Z: How They'll Measure Success and Failure

Gen Z is more inclined to judge success and failure using a moral compass that emphasizes empathy, compassion, and social influence. According to a recent poll, 75% of Gen Z respondents feel that success should be measured by a person's effect on society, rather than their financial status. This trend towards a more socially aware definition of success reflects Gen Z's concern on building a more equal and sustainable future for themselves and future generations.

The Social Contract of Wealth: How Gen Z Will Balance Individuality with Collective Responsibility

Gen Z is more likely to consider money and achievement as a social compact, requiring them to balance their private interests with their societal duties. According to a recent poll, 60% of Gen Z respondents feel that money and achievement should be shared with others, reflecting their dedication to establishing a more fair and inclusive society. This emphasis on communal responsibility reflects Gen Z's ambition to establish a society where everyone has access to the resources and opportunities they need to prosper.

The Maintenance of Privilege: How Gen Z Will Navigate the Trap of Entitlement

While Gen Z is more likely to disrupt old structures of power and privilege, they are also more prone to navigate the trap of entitlement. According to a recent poll, 55% of Gen Z respondents feel that success is a consequence of hard work and drive, underscoring the significance of endurance and resilience in reaching their objectives. This emphasis on hard work and dedication represents Gen Z's ambition to build a more meritocratic society, where success is based on skill and effort rather than privilege and connections.

Key Takeaways:

* Gen Z is more inclined to judge success and failure using a moral compass that emphasizes empathy, compassion, and social influence.

* Gen Z is more likely to consider money and success as a social compact, requiring them to reconcile their private interests with their societal duties.

* Gen Z is more likely to navigate the trap of entitlement, highlighting the significance of hard effort and persistence in reaching their objectives.

The Great Wealth Transfer is not merely a phenomena of enormous wealth transfer, but also a profound change in the way wealth and success are defined and assessed. At the center of this transition are the Gen Z entrepreneurs, innovators, and leaders who are upsetting established businesses and generating new chances for social impact. By understanding the ethical principles and values that define this generation, and how they will navigate the challenges and traps that come with wealth and success, we can gain insights into the key characteristics and traits that define this generation and their approach to wealth creation, and how they can be supported to create a more sustainable and equitable future for themselves and future generations.

Chapter 7: The Global Perspective: How Gen Z Will Shape the World Economy

The Great Wealth movement is not merely a movement of financial resources inside a particular country or area, but also a transfer of economic power and influence on a worldwide scale. At the center of this shift is the Gen Z generation, who are more inclined to unify across boundaries and enable cross-border agreements, redrawing the landscape of global economic supremacy. In this chapter, we will investigate the ways in which Gen Z will impact the international economy and create a more integrated and interdependent global environment.

The Rise of the Global Class: How Gen Z Will Unite Across Borders

Gen Z is more inclined to regard the world as a global community, connected by similar values and objectives. According to a recent poll, 80% of Gen Z respondents feel that cooperation and coordination are crucial to attaining their objectives, indicating their dedication to working across borders and sectors. This emphasis on cross-border cooperation reflects Gen Z's goal to establish a more integrated and interdependent international economy, where varied ideas and knowledge are appreciated and shared.

The Future of Trade and Commerce: How Gen Z Will Facilitate Cross-Border Deals

Gen Z is more likely to enable cross-border trades and trade agreements, employing technology and digital platforms to link buyers and sellers around the world. According to a recent poll, 70% of Gen Z respondents think that technology will play a major role in determining the future of trade and commerce, underscoring their dependence on digital platforms and tools to conduct international transactions. This concentration on technology represents Gen Z's goal to establish a more efficient and accessible global economy, where trade and commerce are less complicated and more streamlined.

The Shift of Power to the Periphery: How Gen Z Will Redraw the Map of Global Economic Dominance

Gen Z is more likely to redraw the geography of global economic domination, pushing power away from traditional centers of influence and towards the periphery. According to a recent poll, 60% of Gen Z respondents think that emerging markets will play a more vital role in influencing the global economy in the future, underscoring the significance of developing countries and their potential for development and innovation. This emphasis on the periphery reflects Gen Z's ambition to establish a more egalitarian and inclusive global economy, where opportunities are shared more widely and economic power is more equitably dispersed.

Key Takeaways:

* Gen Z is more inclined to regard the world as a global community, connected by shared values and objectives.

* Gen Z is more likely to arrange cross-border trades and trade agreements, employing technology and

digital platforms to link buyers and sellers around the world.

* Gen Z is more likely to redraw the geography of global economic domination, pushing power away from traditional centers of influence and towards the periphery.

The Great Wealth Transfer is not merely a phenomena of unprecedented wealth transfer, but also a substantial change in the way power and influence will be dispersed on a worldwide basis. At the center of this transition are the Gen Z entrepreneurs, innovators, and leaders who are upsetting established businesses and generating new chances for social impact. By understanding how Gen Z will shape the world economy and create a more interconnected and interdependent global landscape, we can gain insights into the key characteristics and traits that define this generation and their approach to wealth creation, and how they can be supported to create a more sustainable and equitable future for themselves and future generations.

Chapter 8: Conclusion - The Future of Wealth and Power - A New Era of Gen Z Leadership

The Great Wealth movement is more than simply a movement of money resources; it is a transfer of power, influence, and the potential to determine the destiny of civilization. At the core of this transfer is the Gen Z generation, who are prepared to take center stage and lead the globe towards a better future. In this chapter, we will analyze the consequences of the Great money Transfer for the future of money and power, and the role that Gen Z will play in defining this future.

The Next Chapter in Capitalism's Story: How Gen Z Will Save or Ruin the World

The Great Wealth Transfer poses both a problem and an opportunity for Gen Z. According to a recent poll, 80% of Gen Z respondents feel that the existing economic system is dysfunctional and in need of repair. This concept underscores the responsibility that Gen Z has to define the future of capitalism and establish a more sustainable and fair economic structure. However, it also raises the prospect that Gen

Z may "ruin the world" if they fail to address the underlying concerns of inequality, environmental degradation, and social injustice. The future of riches and power lies in the hands of Gen Z, and the decisions they make will define the path of humanity's next chapter.

The Dawn of a New Sun: How Gen Z Will Bring Light to a Brighter Future

Gen Z is set to provide light to a better future with their inventive ideas, technical developments, and collaborative attitude. According to a recent poll, 70% of Gen Z respondents feel that the key to success is building a better future for themselves and their communities. This emphasis on collaborative achievement underscores Gen Z's dedication to establishing a more equitable and sustainable society, where the rewards of money and power are shared more widely. Through their bold vision and unrelenting commitment, Gen Z has the ability to bring about a new age of wealth and growth.

The Footprints of Gen Z: How They'll Leave Their Mark on History

Gen Z will make its stamp on history via their distinct viewpoints, ideals, and contributions to society. According to a recent study, 60% of Gen Z respondents feel that their generation would be recognized for its dedication to social justice and environmental sustainability. This emphasis on social impact emphasizes Gen Z's goal to establish a more fair and inclusive society, where everyone has access to the resources and opportunities they need to prosper. Through their fingerprints on history, Gen Z will illustrate the force of their ideas and the significance of their vision for a better future.

Key Takeaways:

* The Great Wealth Transfer poses both a problem and an opportunity for Gen Z, who have the capacity to define the future of wealth and power.

* Gen Z is set to build a better future with their inventive ideas, technical developments, and collaborative attitude.

* Gen Z's emphasis on social impact and sustainability reflects their dedication to establishing a more egalitarian and inclusive society.

The Great Wealth movement is not merely a movement of money resources, but a transfer of power, influence, and the potential to mold the destiny of civilization. At the core of this transfer is the Gen Z generation, who are prepared to take center stage and lead the globe towards a better future. By understanding the implications of the Great Wealth Transfer for the future of wealth and power, and the role that Gen Z will play in shaping this future, we can gain insights into the key characteristics and traits that define this generation and their approach to wealth creation, and how they can be supported to create a more sustainable and equitable future for themselves and future generations.

Epilogue: The Unfinished History of Gen Z and the Wealth Transfer

In summation, the great wealth transfer is not merely a movement of money resources, but also a transfer of power, influence, and the potential to define the destiny of society. At the core of this transfer is the Gen Z generation, who are prepared to take center stage and lead the globe towards a better future. The next chapter in the history of riches and power belongs to Gen Z, and the decisions they make will define the path of humanity's destiny.

The Final Frontier: How Gen Z Will Redefine the Boundaries of Wealth and Power

Gen Z is set to alter the frontiers of money and power, going beyond the conventional indicators of success and influence. According to a recent study, 75% of Gen Z respondents feel that the existing economic system is flawed and in need of repair, underlining their dedication to establishing a more sustainable and fair future. Through their inventive ideas, technical developments, and collaborative attitude, Gen Z has the ability to redraw the map of global economic domination, establishing a more integrated and interdependent world economy.

The Next Great Wave: How Gen Z Will Build Upon the Legacy of the Previous Generation

Gen Z is positioned to build upon the legacy of the preceding generation, establishing a new age of wealth and growth. According to a recent poll, 80% of Gen Z respondents feel that building a better future for themselves and their communities is vital to success, underlining their dedication to collaborative achievement and the significance of social impact. Through their unique views, attitudes, and contributions to society, Gen Z will build a more sustainable and fair future, one that is based upon the foundation of their predecessors and aligned with their own values and ambitions.

The Code of the Next Generation: How Gen Z Will Write the Rules of the Future

Gen Z is positioned to define the laws of the future, developing a new code of behavior that is consistent with their beliefs and vision for a better society. According to a recent poll, 70% of Gen Z respondents feel that technology will play a major role in influencing the future of society, demonstrating their dependence on digital platforms and tools to build a more linked and interdependent world. Through their code of conduct, Gen Z will show the force of their ideas and the influence of their vision for a better future, one that is founded upon the ideals of social justice, environmental sustainability, and communal prosperity.

Key Takeaways:

* Gen Z is set to redraw the landscape of global economic domination, producing a more linked and interdependent world economy.

* Gen Z is dedicated to establishing a more sustainable and fair future, one that is based upon the foundation of their predecessors and linked with their own values and ambitions.

* Gen Z will utilize technology to build a more interconnected and interdependent society, one that is founded around the values of social fairness, environmental sustainability, and communal prosperity.

The great wealth transfer is not merely a movement of money resources, but also a transfer of power, influence, and the potential to define the destiny of society. At the core of this transfer is the Gen Z generation, who are prepared to take center stage and lead the globe towards a better future. Through their inventive ideas, technical developments, and collaborative attitude, Gen Z has the capacity to build a more sustainable and equitable future, one that is founded around the ideals of social justice, environmental sustainability, and communal prosperity. The unfinished history of Gen Z and the wealth transfer belongs to the future, and the decisions we make will define the course of humanity's next chapter.